Hamza Hussain (hvmz.h) - 1

This book is for

Aima

Laboni

and Saikha.

if it wasn't for these people,
this book wouldn't be in your palms.

Contents

LIFE

Life... is a mystery in itself. It leaves you with the illusion of love; it leaves you seeing better days. But when you open your eyes the very next time, it's all bleeding out from your very veins.

Life

The thing I learnt about life was that people, circumstances and chances will always come in different lights. The darkness… and the light. What took me a very long time to learn what they truly showed, shouldn't have taken me that long. The answer was always in front of my eyes. The thing I learnt about the light and the darkness… it was how they showed you. You are made of darkness and the light. The light being your positivity, your emotions and your ability to see things how they are; whereas the darkness shows your inner strength. Your divine emotions, the side you never show to anyone else. Which is why sometimes when things don't go your way, it's just not your time yet. The universe needs time to match its light and darkness with yours.

Life

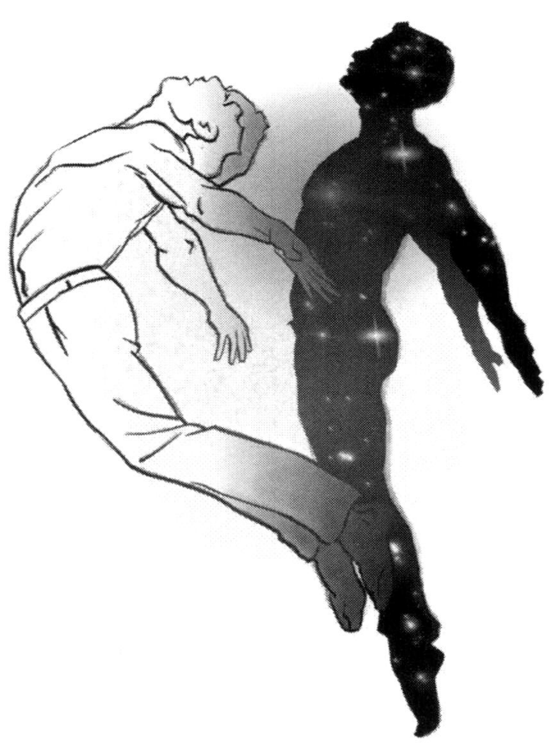

Things happen, life goes on. Life is a choice that we have, we have opportunities to die every day, we have the choice to ignore that and look over the deathly initiatives and look at the lively situations. It's contradictory how we have the choice to die whenever we please, but continue living as though we don't think about it every day. We live life with death in our palms; we die with death flowing through our body.

Life

Most people like to believe that things happen for a reason. What if it wasn't, what if you wanted it to be how you wanted it, you're just in the process of it getting either better or worse?

Life

Chances are given to those who deserve them. Chances turn into opportunities and opportunities turn into finished results and consequences. The better prepared you are for the unseen future, the better chance you have of attaining a good life, a life that we think will be beneficial for us in the long run.

Life

Maybe life is a puzzle that only you could solve. The things that happen, the choices you make, the voices you hear, the voices you ignore are all yourself. One big puzzle that can only be solved by all the pieces coming together, one by one.

Life

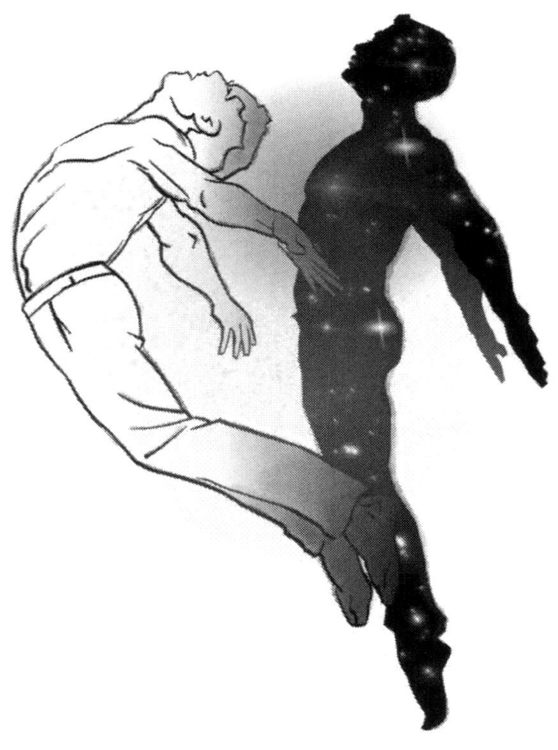

Sometimes you have to let things flow, let things go their natural way. Things never work out when they're forced, the love's not in there anymore. It's like a long bumpy road to a place where things will never go right.

Life

maybe life

has its

own ways

of telling

you when

something's

wrong.

it

teaches us

who we

really are,

careless lovers

or just

fools

playing along.

Life

Life shows us that sometimes we find the answers in the most absurd ways possible. We find things we didn't necessarily need to find out, and never find out the things we wanted to find out. It's almost like searching the world for a treasure, only to give up, and it land at your front door the next day. It's meeting right people at the wrong times, it's learning more about the people around you, the things they'd never tell you. Life.. Is a discovery in itself, it's a mystery solved only by time, and that time is a lesson in itself that leaves you impatient, wanting and waiting for more. For the more you pursue it, the less you'll receive.

Life

if it's

one thing

i've learnt

about life

it's that

things are

meant to be

left alone,

to grow.

to build.

to empower.

to learn.

Life

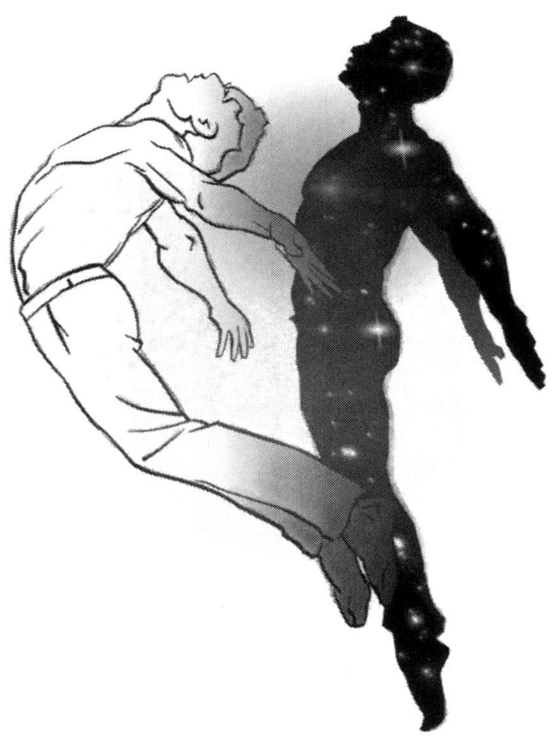

Too often we forget that at the end of something horrible, something beautiful starts. The relief we feel when bad energy goes away, can only be beaten by something even more extraordinary, something more powerful waiting for us, to explore, to find ourselves within the uncertainty of the future.

Life

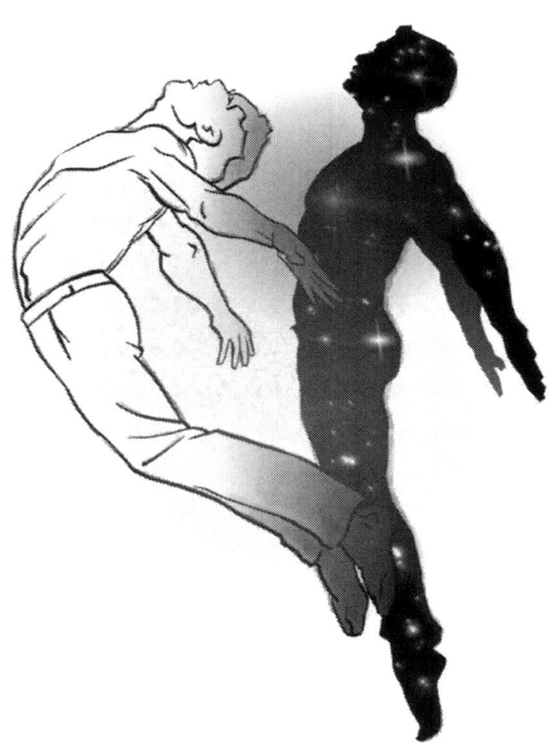

In life, the people we love return to him, someone who loves the people we love, more. Realise that it's for the greater good, there's no such thing as the right or wrong timing, it's all about chances and circumstances. The people who leave us, earlier than you thought, are the ones that would want you to live, laugh and love for them. Don't spend time crying and holding yourself back from the inevitable, for time goes and flies further and further each second, and each second you spend lingering in the past, is a second wasted of you becoming a better you. A person your loved one would've always wanted you to be.

Life

things

are

meant

to be.

never stress

about anything

you cannot

control,

you are

mixing your

energy

with a

different kind,

a different force

that has never

touched yours.

Life

Sometimes life won't make sense. You'll be put in circumstances out of your control, with people you never thought you'd see, with situations out of your control. And sometimes you can't see a way out of it; it looks like all hope is lost. It feels like a boulder blocking every route you have to escape. But imagine yourself at a train station. You have the choice to jump onto the tracks, or to savour life, see what you can really do. I want you to imagine walking to the end of the train stop, right where the station ends. Look into the horizon; look so deep that the train tracks fade away into the light of the sky. And as you see that, look at how the two parallel train tracks meet. If anything they ever taught me in maths class, it was that anything parallel would never meet, but if you ever looked at train tracks from a different angle, you'd see that they join into one.

-perspective.

Life

With life, comes risks. With risks, comes adventure. With adventures, come incredible stories to tell. We live for us, we live to become people we could look back at, and see that our life that was worth living, was lived to the fullest. Life that was about doing what you love, doing something different, getting out of your comfort zone. Don't you think that it's time that something changed, that void in your life needed filling? That your Mondays were something actually worth looking forward to, not dreading them? The way you make the most out of life is by spending those Fridays to find better stories to tell on Mondays, instead of life making the most out of you by making you climb each day like it were a ladder to hell.

Life

Expectations can kill a man, deeper than a wound from the sharpest knife, or the bitterness from the strongest poison. You see, it's not what you think it is, but the thing is, if you lived a life waiting for something to happen... Would it happen? Would it have been as good as you thought it would've been?

Life

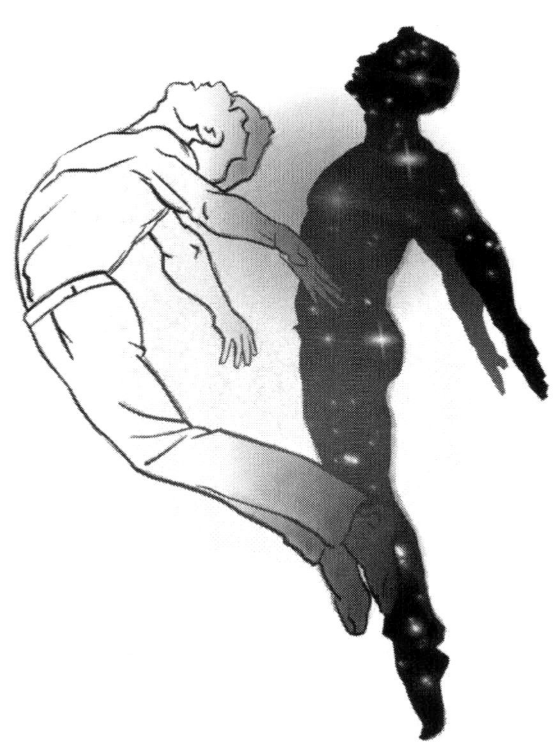

It's funny how the past can change your future. Things that happen in the past, change what happens in the future. Memories, for instance. Memories are bought back every now and then whenever our minds drift away into random thoughts. You'll think about all the bad memories more than the good ones. Those bad memories are toxic to you. They're simply a reminder for you to not make the same mistake again, and do better in its place. Think about something in your past that you just can't let go. Why? It's because this is the closest you can get to a certain point in time where you felt like the world was yours. Memories can also torture you mentally. Anytime, anywhere. Whether you're running in the park or listening to music, something will always remind you of the bad memories causing you to just fall victim... and feel worthless.

Life

The world will throw you suffering in ways you'd never thought you'd see, in ways you never thought you'd feel. The world will throw you roses, in illusion of something beautiful- when the thorns are pricking your fingers with every touch. The thing with life is that it's a metaphor, a symbolisation of a reminder that nothing good, ever comes easy. In every struggle, you see depth of beauty, in every outcome, you see a difference. Why do you think love in itself, brings more out of people than they ever saw in themselves?

Life

The colours
of life
are shown to
us by the way
we look at them.
the more you paint
life as a brighter
picture
the more it
stands out.
the darker you shade
it down,
the more it provokes
meaning; depth.
and that's the
beauty of life..
the colours
are more than
what you
see.

Life

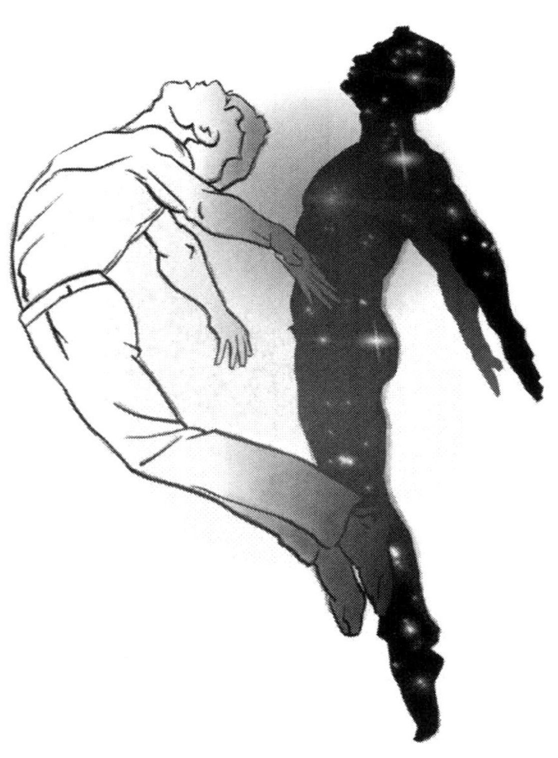

The end of all things comes eventually
you cannot blame something
that wasn't ever in
the palms of your soul
when you know you
could've saved something
so beautiful from stopping;
the beauty was preserved,
and the idea lives forever.

People

You see, the thing with people, is that they come and go. You can never be certain that someone's going to stay in your life forever. But.. There'll always be people that make you feel like that, they'll make you feel at home, where you feel safe. Where danger cannot harm a hair on your head, but can damage what's inside of it. And these people will always leave you asking yourself the same question; what is it about me that makes them want to stay? Sometimes they'll answer that question for you, but what you really need is your approval. You need to know what it is about you that makes people want to share a home inside your head, you need to know what it is about you... that makes your house a home.

People

We are just the perfect strangers, to an anonymous world. We are the life, the structure of society itself. Why do we fear ourselves, why do we hate ourselves? We... breathe the same air. We see the same sky. We live for the freedom we desire, but our freedoms are limited in the eyes of others, and maybe that's why we don't feel good enough to see the vision of our own freedom, we chase someone else's. We chase someone else's freedom, live a lie with the truth of another; we sabotage the freedom we desired, with the hatred of a better freedom in sight. Sometimes in life, we forget chasing what matters to us, because of what someone else has shown you; a ***better vision****. And that's where we go wrong, what we desire will always be what we desire, and no matter how big or small someone else's vision will be, nothing will compare to yours. A vision you call home.*

People

A Bouquet Laced With Liquor

too often

we place

happiness

in the hands

of the same people

that hold

the blade to

rip it apart.

~

too less

we desire the

absence of

people

that can

leave

just as

easily, we deny

our lives

for them

to stay.

People

*I always used to live life, with an imaginary image, a polaroid with a thread running through my mind with a picture of what I always wanted, what kind of person I wanted in my life. I always had faith that there'd be someone, at least someone who came close. I mean, 7 billion people, there'd **HAVE** to be someone at least close to it, right? Days, weeks, months and years flew by, no one ever came close. I was called selfish, I expected too much, or I was just immature. I always thought about what it was like to be immature, think about it, what's the first thing to ever come to your head when it comes to the word 'immature'? A kid, right? And something I always lived by... was to always talk to the inner kid in me, it's what keeps our sparks alive, it's what keeps us... us. What I learned though, is that it's okay to be wanting something, having standards too high is better than having standards too low. However, life's common principle proves to us, that sometimes when we aim too high, we fall too low. And when we fall low, through suffering is where we find the strength to fully pick ourselves up. It's okay to bend your own rules, it's just knowing who for.*

People

He has to adapt
he has to stay the way society has
moulded the main figure to maintain.
He is meant to be a cold body.

What if he wanted to express himself?
What if he wanted to show his true feelings?
Would it make him less of a man?
Would it make him less masculine?

She has to keep up

With society, the media

Stripped of her emotions, her interests

To be a rebirth of an unsolicited person, a body

Only left for show.

What if she wanted to be herself?

What if she wanted to be... happy?

What if her happiness didn't make her weak?

Would it change the way you look at her?

People

People leave memories, imprints of their footsteps in your mind. Imagine people worked for you, in your mind. They had roles; they did something that contributed to your mind working accordingly, a cog with another cog, rotating and working together to just make things better. And what happens is that one day, the cogs stop working. They stop moving, to make the mechanism of ***you*** *work. The oil, the grease that keeps the movement smooth, it runs dry. Sometimes there's no more ointment to keep it going, so you have to throw out a part, or it just stops working. You have to throw out parts, you have to throw out that exact model, and find another, a better one. One that works properly. But you won't ever forget the first one you ever had, because that would be absurd, the model of the cog that helped make you work... would be the one that makes you see things differently, makes you work differently than another one will. What I'm trying to say is that some parts can be replaced, they can be exchanged, they can be swapped. But sometimes the part works so good that it just changes everything, and that's the good we always look for, the good that changes us. That's kind of why it's almost impossible to forget people that have done certain things for you.*

People

we give

people

the parts

of us

that

made us

who we

are.

now

we're just

people

who don't remember

who

or what

we were,

just broken pieces

of a shattered

masterpiece.

People

We've all heard that saying before, 'No one knows what's behind the tears of a clown'. Fact is, we do. We think that they find pride in making other people laugh to make them feel better about themselves, when in reality, that person is being broken down each and every day, thinking about others happiness and laughter compared to their very own. It's a mystery how people can stay sane, yet seem happy when you ask them what's wrong.

People

Cutting people off is not a bad thing. It is never a bad thing. When you realise that certain people are toxic to you or are just in your life serving no purpose, you do not need that excess stress. Even if it's without warning, do it.

People

I've had this theory in mind for a while, if a person wants to be a part of your life, they'll make an effort to actually be in it. If you find yourself forcing them to stay, you're only making yourself look weak. You're only inviting them to hurt you more, harder even.

People

the love

you relentlessly

push towards

other people

who have

love within

different people

can never be

replaced,

only ever

mistaken for

kindness,

which people

will take

and take

and take

until you

have no

choice but

to turn

cold.

-love towards others, rather than yourself

People

I've always seen that less was always more, when the words I spoke, the people I chose to stay with, were always more than what I needed, more than what I wanted. The less people I chose, the more I felt isolated, the more people I chose, the more I felt lonely. It was always a battle between burdening people with my presence, or people burdening me without theirs. It was only then that I realised that being by myself, I'd realise what it truly meant to be alone. What it truly would mean, to fall in love with my own company, as compared to the self-lingering thought of sticking onto a person that would one day brush me off... like it was nothing.

People

you should

never have

to seek

yourself

in people

that aren't

sure

if they belong

to the world

or to

themselves.

People

*you see people that you think have it all together;
their world's a complete success to you. but even
then, stars feel alone when the moon isn't there.*

People

The beauty of friendships is that they last either a short time, or a lifetime. A life with an everlasting friendship is a life with stability and consistency, a vibe you don't get much nowadays. A lifetime friendship isn't determined by the amount of time you've known someone, rather it's the thought of having someone you can rely on and have someone there who hasn't ever let you down since you met them. It's a person who's seen your faults and your flaws and has always saw you for who you are. A friendship shows so much about a person, by how open they are, or if their effort isn't consistent. The difference between a short friendship and a lifetime is the fact that in an everlasting friendship, the trust is built on a foundation of the friendship you show. The shorter friendships tend to have a split second connection then the rest is a question of mystery and how you perceive the trust within yourself rather than someone else.

-we want a friendship that lasts a lifetime, but aren't willing to put in a lifetime.

People

You'll see the colours of the people that choose to show their life in the way they try to manoeuvre their instincts. That way, you see who's predictable and who is, and who isn't. The colours of a person that's predictable, tend to paint pictures of and imagine in your mind whereas a person whose colours were in black and white will leave you in the depths of their mystery trying to figure out their next move.
A person wanting to be in your life wouldn't be predictable, which is when the paint is mixed, you get a different colour of different shades.

People

love
is what
we search
for
in people
but forget that
love from ourselves
shows us how much we're worth
and how much we're
capable of when
we think
of love.

People

In people we see good or we see bad. It's almost like judging someone but it's kind of different. It's looking at someone and thinking about what lies within, we automatically assume what a person must be about, because of the way they dress. But in reality, people walk around with something different on the outside and something the same on the inside. It's truly believed that a person reflects who they are by what they do, but we don't really know how much of a weight a person's carrying on the inside that we see light on the outside. Misconceptions create assumptions, and assumptions create a character.

People

In life, we click with people like we've seen them before, which in reality, we haven't. It's almost like that feeling where you recognise someone that caught your eye in a room filled with people which only ever bought a vibe that felt like you knew each other in a different life. It's almost like an instant connection with how your bodies feel, how your mind feels. . . it's like a higher common energy that you both possess.

People

when you
allow
certain people
in your life to
see the
flaws
the dark side
the lows
your deep thoughts
the lessons you
learn,
the distance you
throw and
the emotions
swirling around your
beautiful mind
and still hope
for them to
stay

that is trust.

Love

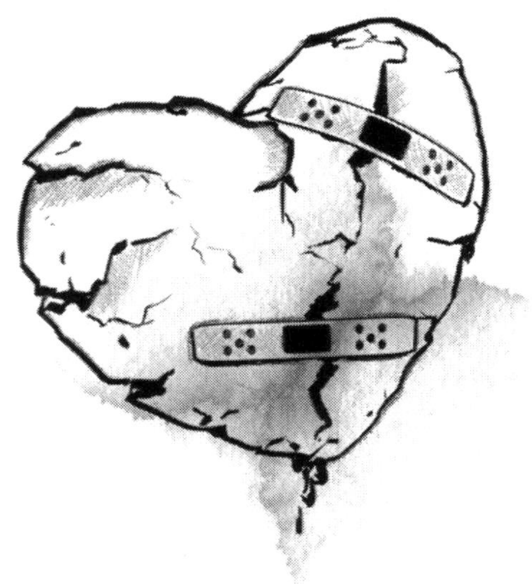

People think that a relationship is just love, giving someone flowers, taking them to the movies and kissing in the rain. What if I told you, they're right, but just not for the right reasons? Relationships are ugly, they're beautiful. They're beautifully ugly, there's so many more emotions in a relationship than just love, although it's how you show them that makes it all worthwhile. You want to show love, you tell them how much. You want to show love, you listen to their favourite song and you find out why, what words and what verse is their favourite, why it plays strings with the veins of their heart, why it makes them feel a certain way. You want to show love? Show it in everything you do, even the things you thought you'd never do.

love

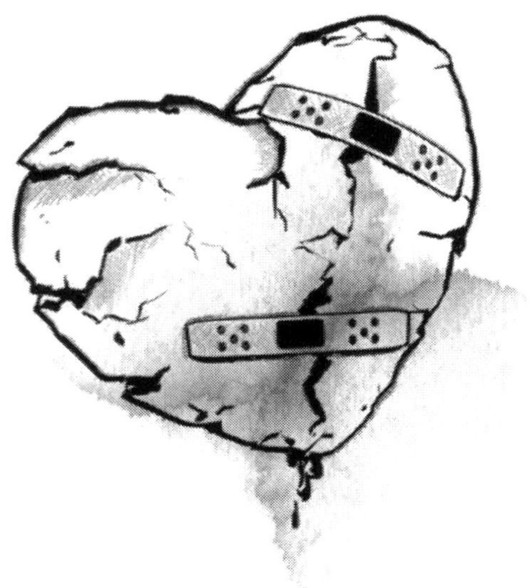

we wish to be held, when we just want to stay
warm
we want to never let go of ourselves
but we hunt for the feeling
in other people to treat us better
than sometimes the way we treat ourselves..
luckily enough, we find that someone in another
body,
or we realise it was us.. all along.

love

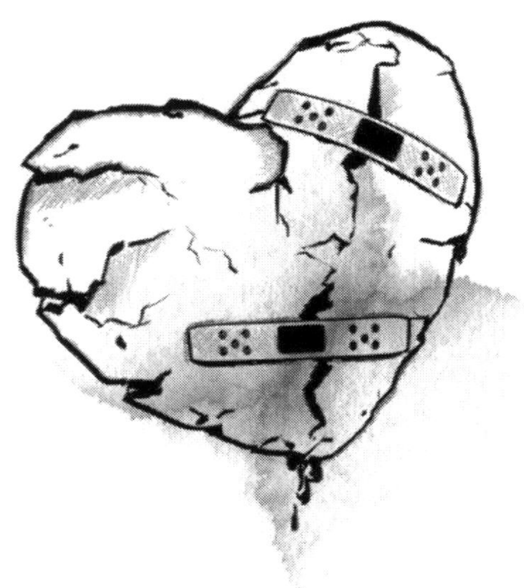

There will always be doubt
even though you tell yourself
there isn't
there will be a little ounce of
trust
that just doesn't want to join
hands with the rest of your emotions
sometimes you think
it's too good to be true
and sometimes you'll think
that you give so much of yourself
that sometimes being greedy
is your way of being selfish.
Because once upon a time
you gave all your trust
and where did it get you?
Regret. We can't all let go of our fears
when they're the things
waking us up.

love

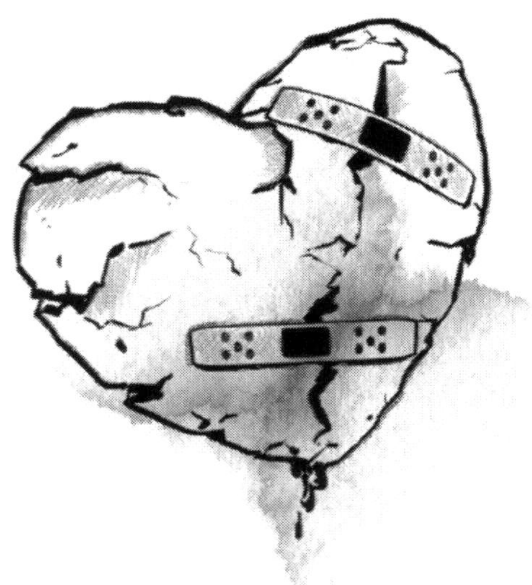

gravity holds you down
more than you think
physically is what you learn in classrooms
mentally is what you learn yourself
but it tends to let you
float sometimes
where you need someone to hold you down
where you feel home
and free.

love

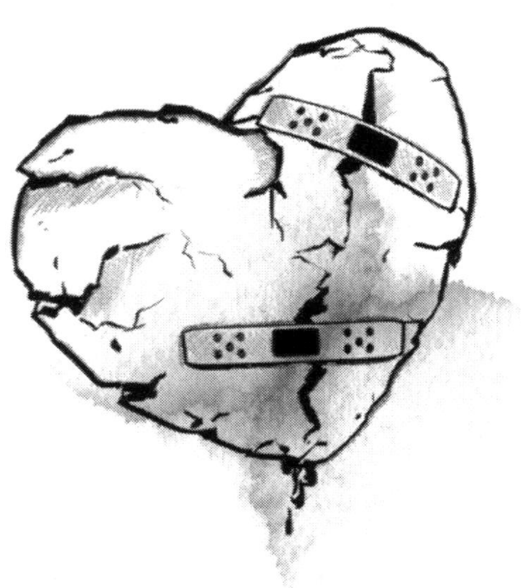

Life is a tie of balances
where everything is
almost never the same
where the sea
wouldn't be the sea
without the shore
or the way
the sky meets
the land.
It's never the same effort
that's given back
but whatever you give
you'll get back
more or less
than what you expected;
love is like that.
There will be days where
you give a quarter of your mind
to someone who wants to
give you three quarters of
theirs.
It's never the same.

love

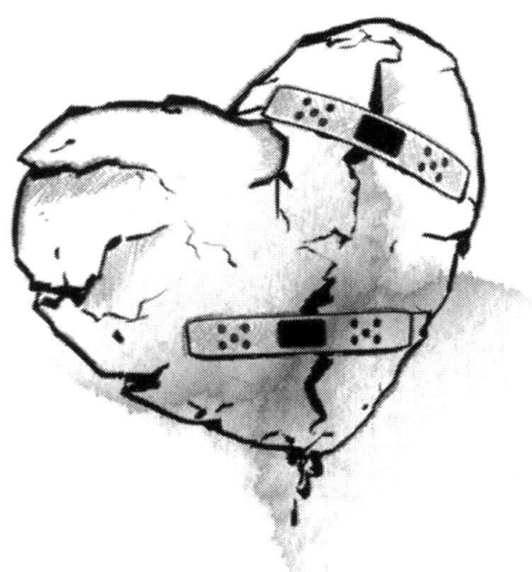

There is a love that we crave, the perfect kind of love. That love we imagine in our minds, that love which is the point you'd be the most happiest if it ever happened. It's that certain kind of love that sets the benchmark for everything that you've ever felt, and that love will only be quenched when you think that something similar or better comes along.

love

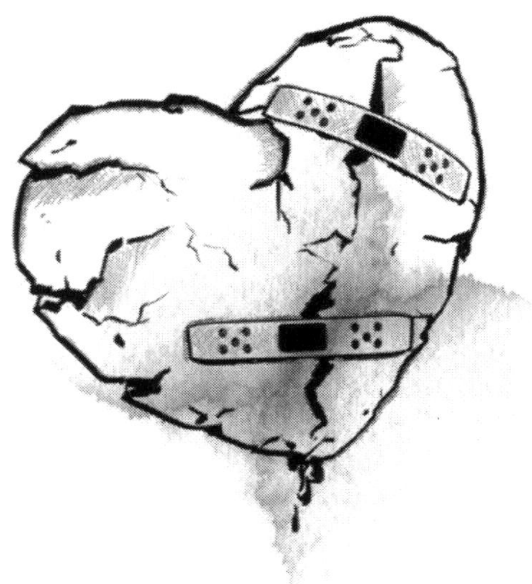

there is a
lot more
to love
than just
sex
when
a body grows
old and
tired
of constant
melodies,
it's the mind
that rides your brainwaves
strokes your demons
and plays with your
angels
kisses your
thoughts
and caresses your
dreams.

love

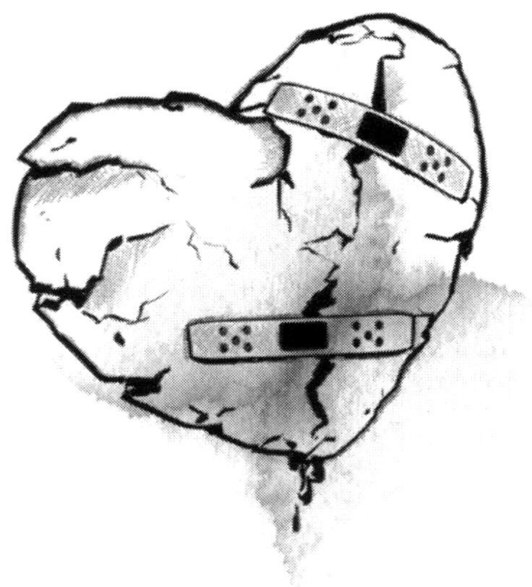

you feel like
love is your
escape
from the toxic
waste your life
throws in your
face,
you find a home
where you feel
comfortable
with the
way you
see the damage,
maybe that's why you
love *love* *a lot*
it makes your house
a home.

love

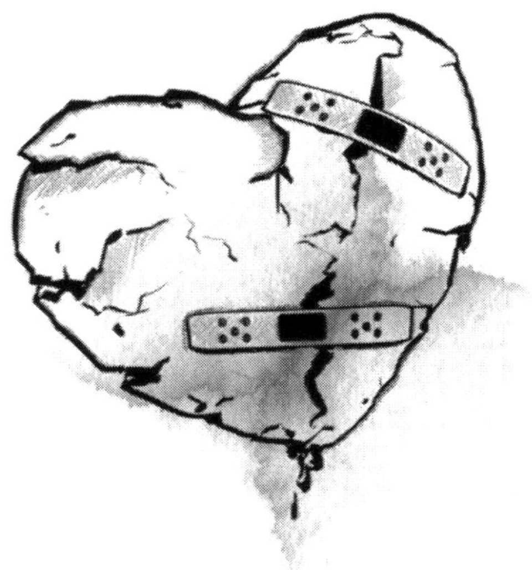

There are so many emotions and how they make you feel. There are families in our minds that feel like distant people that we rarely see. We rarely see happiness, as it's always with love, we see sadness every day but it's always hanging out with fear and depression. We tend to become the equivalent of the people we hang around with, the people we surround ourselves with, the emotions were the only people I talked to, I always fell victim to the bullying by sadness.

love

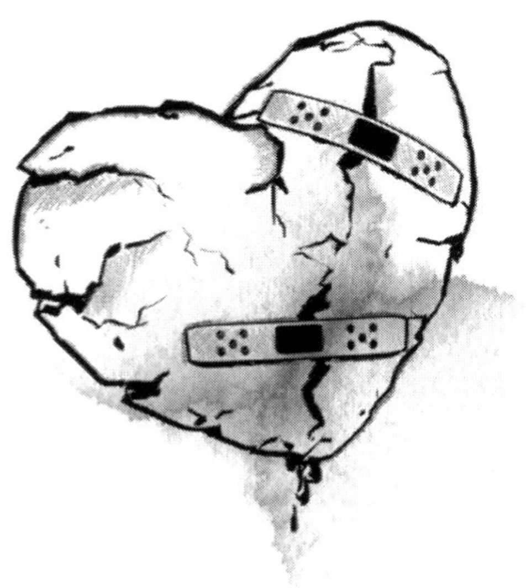

Love is like a trap you don't want to fall into, but you find yourself pushing you in anyway. You're always the one putting the gun to your temple and pulling the trigger to let your blood, thoughts and feeling splatter all over the walls. You tell yourself 'never again' but you always find yourself getting attached to something that's not yours.

Imagine literally having the power to self-destruct, but there's something holding you back. Someone holding you back. Someone who knows that it's better for you to throw away all your anger and built up emotions at them, just so they know you feel better.
That's how you know it's true, when that someone wants better for you, than you want for yourself.

love

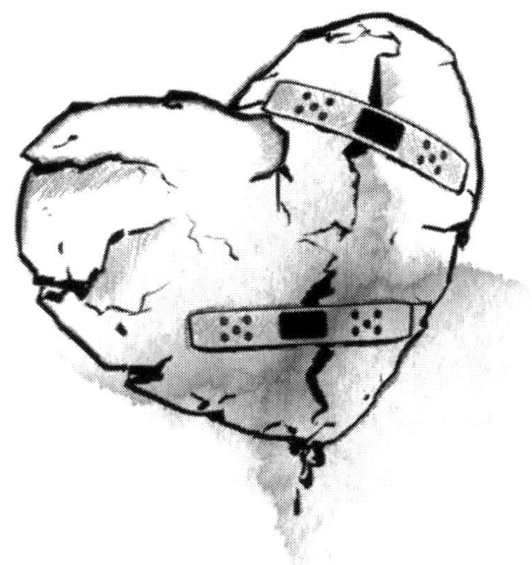

Have you ever fallen in love with someone so hard that their every emotion became yours? You felt whatever they felt? The way you'd feel jealous and unappreciated when you saw them talking to someone with a better conversation flow than yours would tear you up inside? And what could you do to cover it up? Act like it doesn't matter. Act like you're not bothered by it, like it's a normal thing. Put on a fake smile and continue with your day just internally shattering into tiny pieces at the thought of that person with someone else. Ever loved someone that you forgot about everything and everyone around you, just had eyes and ears for that one person? Ever had a love so unique that it could only be understood by you two? No one in the world could understand it, only you two? That itself is the mystery of love, the art. The art of being at peace, or being in pieces.

love

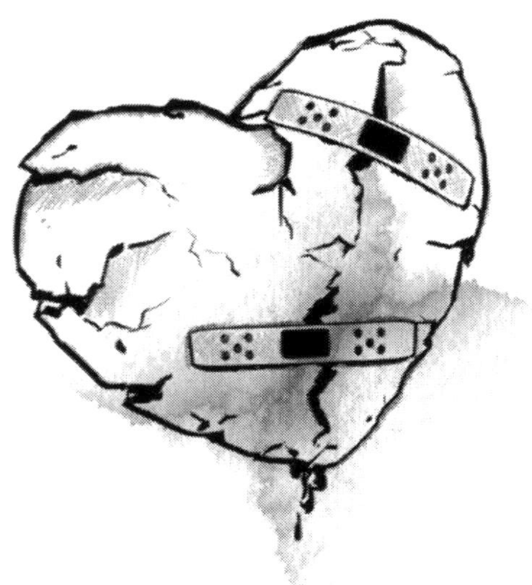

*there is no such thing as a replacement for love.
there is only a lack of effort. an artificial rose will
never be alive like a real one would.*

love

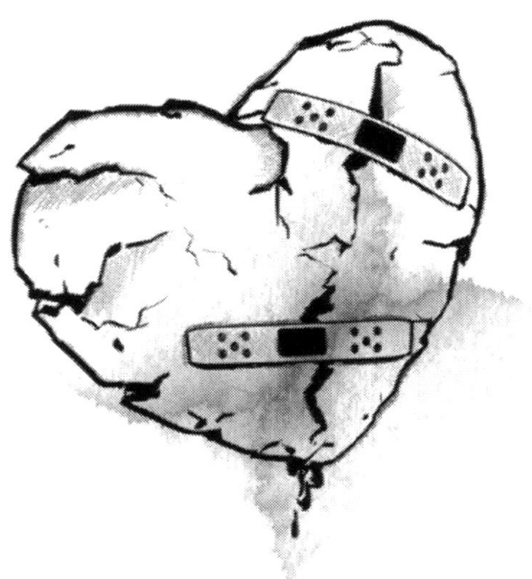

Maybe, there was a point where you loved that special someone so much, you'd break every bone in your body for their happiness. Maybe, when they didn't realise your love for them wasn't enough, you resorted to doing things you don't normally do for them.. Maybe, when that person broke you so bad, the pieces of your heart were so tiny and brittle, it was impossible to mend them together. Maybe then you looked for this love you wanted back, elsewhere... And when you found it... You didn't know how to react. The three words you've wanted to hear for so long, play like strings in your mind... By the first person to break you. You're too scared to linger back into that area of your mind, so you look for that love again, but with a different person to see if the strings in your mind and heart will play a different melody. It's a constant cycle.

love

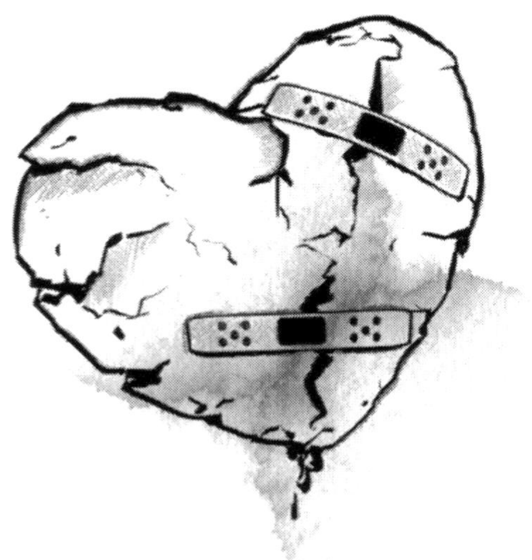

Love cannot be bought. Love isn't money, it isn't a big house or a flashy car. It has to be nurtured, it has to be taken care of. It's like a tree, you plant a seed, you water it and make sure it gets sunlight. Imagine the seed as yourself, or someone you value highly. The water is the communication and the sunlight is the effort. You fall in love with the way you communicate, you fall in love with the effort, there's nothing better than watching something grow into something beautiful. Things take time, rushed things only leave you lazier, they leave you with more problems, whereas things you grow, things you nurture... They last a lifetime in your heart.

love

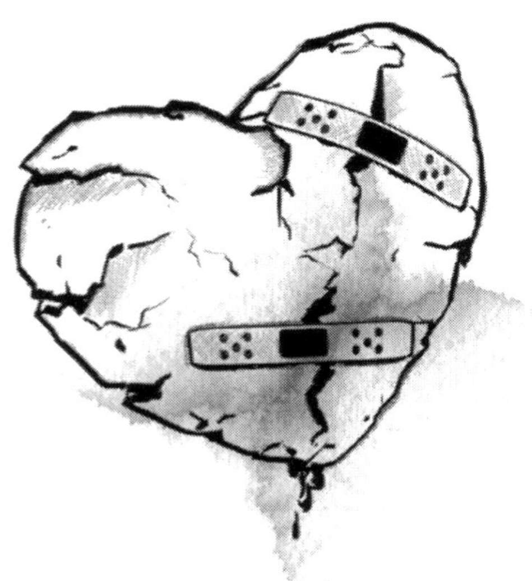

I believe that in love, 'effort' doesn't play a role. You could bend over backwards, turn ice into flames, or jump off a high building and survive. Yet, the other person would be happy, but deep down, they'd be looking for a spark they couldn't light with you. Just know if it was meant to be, it was.

love

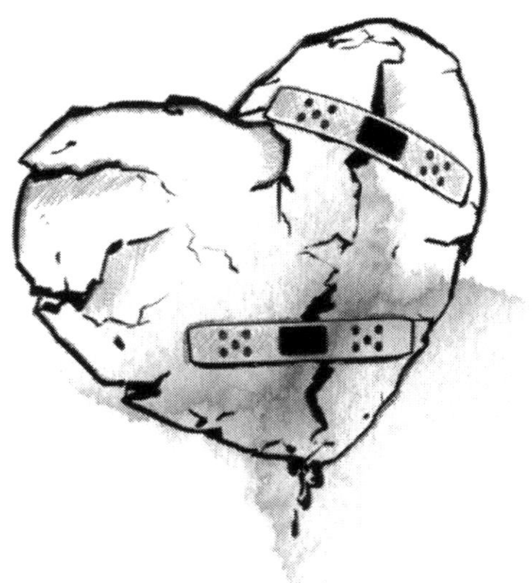

I wish that you find
the love you searched for
all your life
in the palms of your hands
or in the palms of someone
else's, you deserve the world
and everything beautiful in it
like the sound of the wind
blowing through your fingers
and the sun looking into your
eyes.

-one day.

love

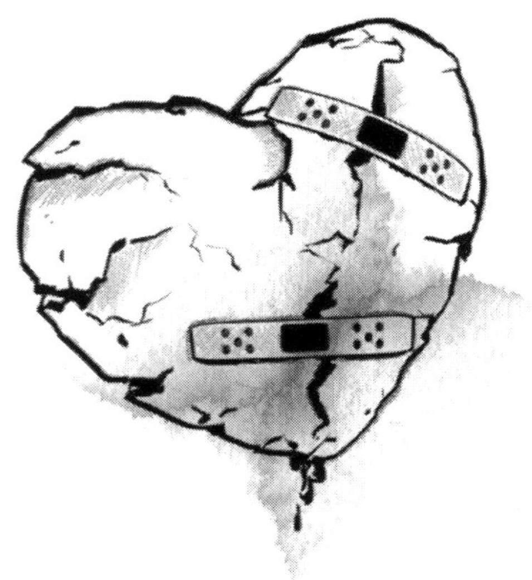

my mind
wanders and
it finds peace
in your soul.

-freedom

love

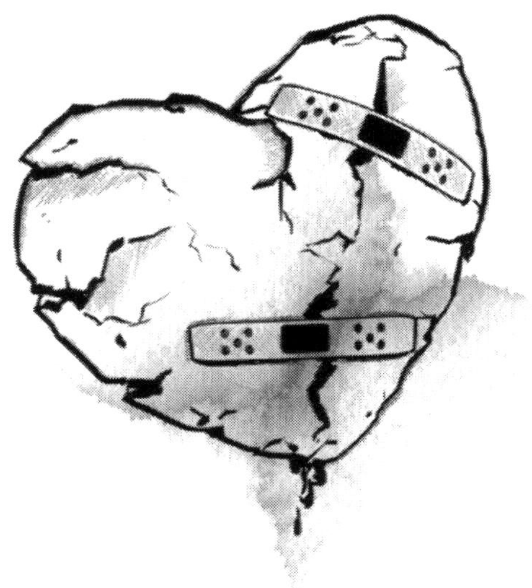

It's funny how
I went from never believing in love
to falling into it again
like an abyss
a vortex
that I could never escape from.;
love was a trap that
I tried to escape
but no matter how much I escaped
to more it found me
collapsed in a hotel room
at 5am in the morning
struggling to sleep.
that was when
I realised that
I couldn't run anymore
I couldn't walk
I couldn't talk
I was a prisoner to my own heart
that corrupted my mind
with the illusions of peace
in the heart of
another.

love

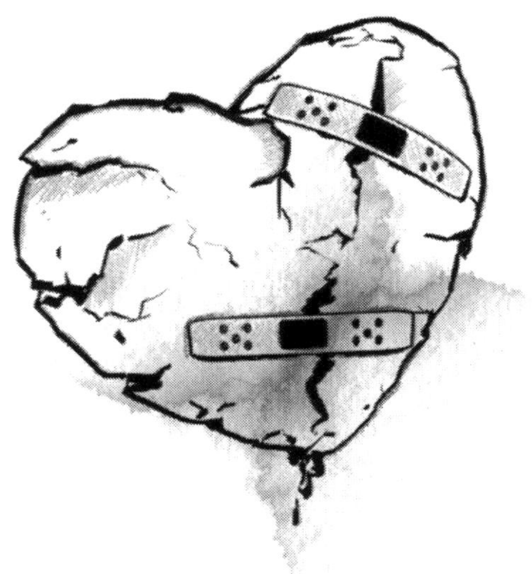

the same way
an artist falls in love
with the world
the same way a writer
cannot speak what the heart
hides
or the same way a singer lets the emotions
linger in the notes of their voices
was the effect you had
on the world
you didn't realise
the beauty in your soul
that even when captured
would live forever
but never be like you.

-original

love

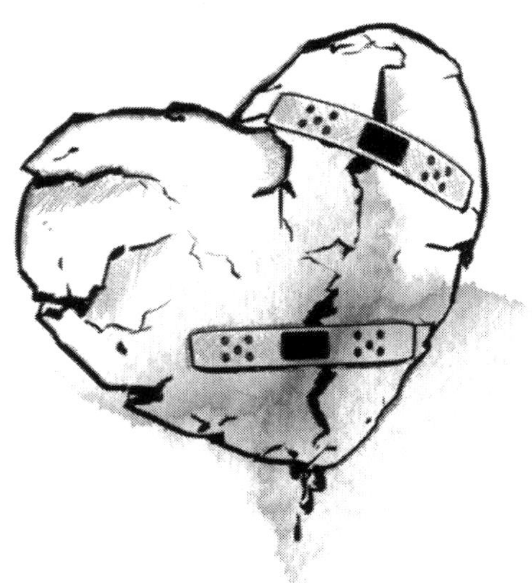

when the flaws disappear
the negatives turn to positives
the scars heal
the wounds close
they become perfect
like they were perfect
all their lives
and normal was something
they never knew
you forget yourself
and wonder how a person
makes you feel lucky
that all you saw in your eyes
was the best thing you
ever witnessed.

Hurt

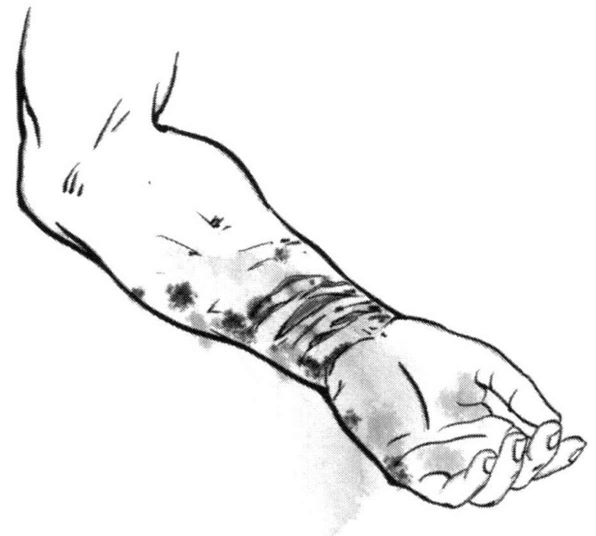

You feel like
the world has
split into two
and the hurricanes
are nothing but rainbows
with a pot of disappointment
waiting at the end of the line..
you feel like the world is sinking deeper
into the space it floats around in
and you feel so alone
you feel like you don't matter
you feel like a speck of
dust that can be wiped
away just as easy..
but nothing would
ever be how it
is without
you.

Hurt

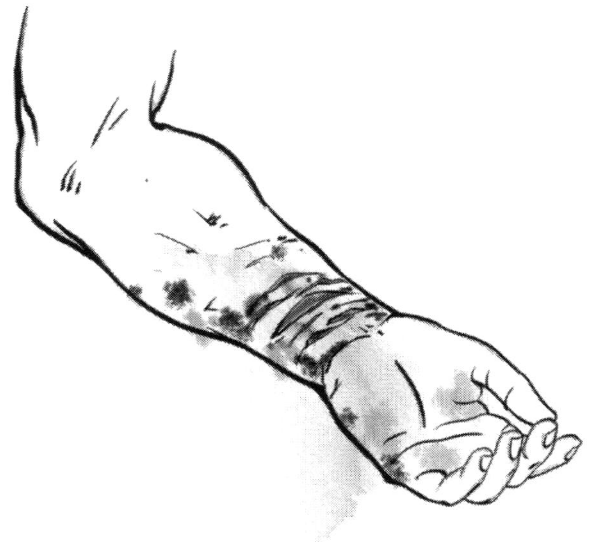

It hurts, I know it does. But you don't seem to like it; you don't seem to dislike it either. You feel that ignoring the pain will only make it worse, and you feel like facing it will only make you fall in love with it. We're uncertain of what we need to do, hide from our pain, or to tend the beast that haunts our nightmares, the tormentor of our minds. But sometimes we need to see further than the cages we're locked up in, we need to see that it's temporary. The beauty of pain is that it never lasts, but the moments it begins, on god; will be the most confusing thing you've ever experienced. You'll feel a thousand questions with the sharpness of a million thorns beat against your heart, mocking the way it beats, as if it were to live a false life. The hurt will force you to pack your bags and run far away from who you used to be.. Into something stronger. Something harder.

Hurt

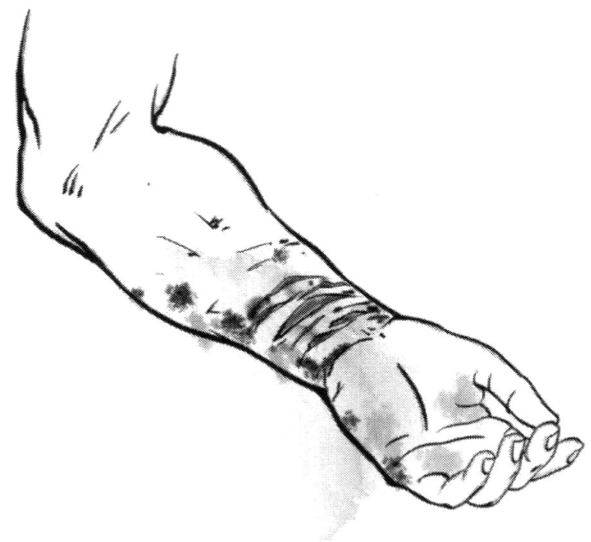

Sometimes keeping something in and letting it reach the deepest corners of your body feels better than releasing tsunamis that seem to drown other people as well as yourself.

Hurt

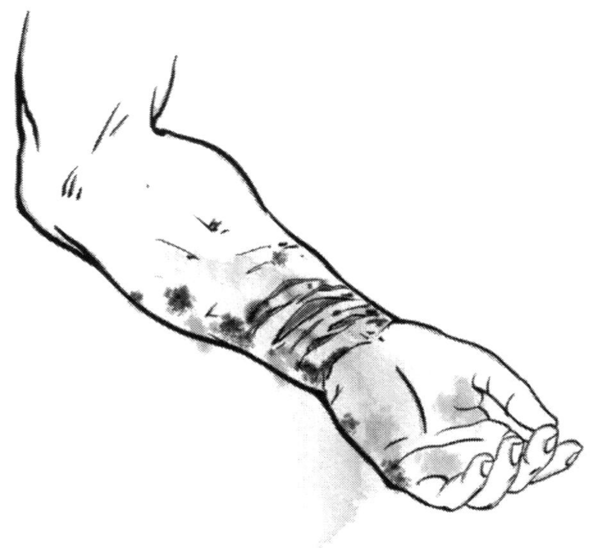

Flowers don't wither the same anymore, they have a lot more meaning now. You thought that they died because there was no more rain, there was no more sunlight, they changed colours and started to die. The sun doesn't seem to set like it did, you don't miss the sun anymore, you live in the dark. You find a home in the darkness even the light couldn't find. You become familiar with the darkness, you don't ever want to get out, the feeling of security fills you up… and takes you in.

Hurt

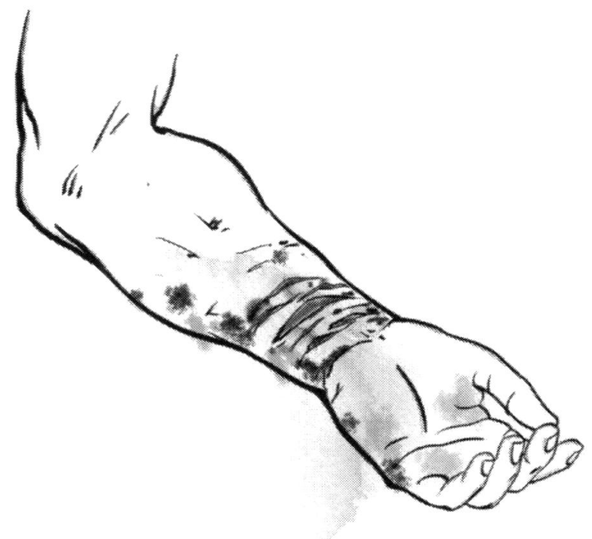

We are hurt all too often by the things that are in control... but we dwell over the things that weren't- we blame ourselves for it instead of realising it was the universe determining a power between two forces that were too strong to last.

Hurt

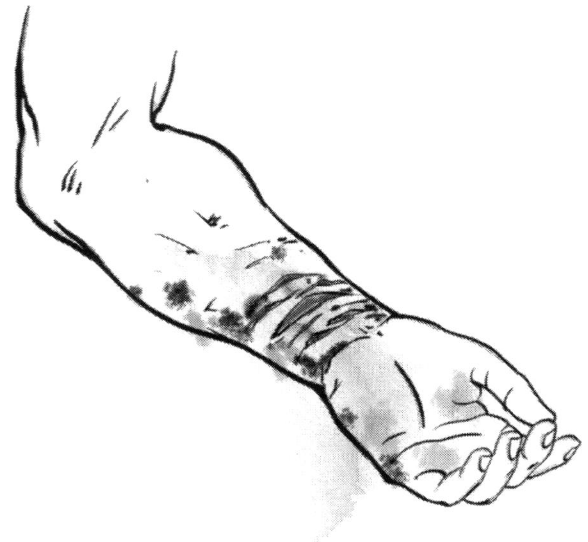

..a part of me hurts everyday but i just ignore it, it's just pain that's there to remind me i'm still alive.

Hurt

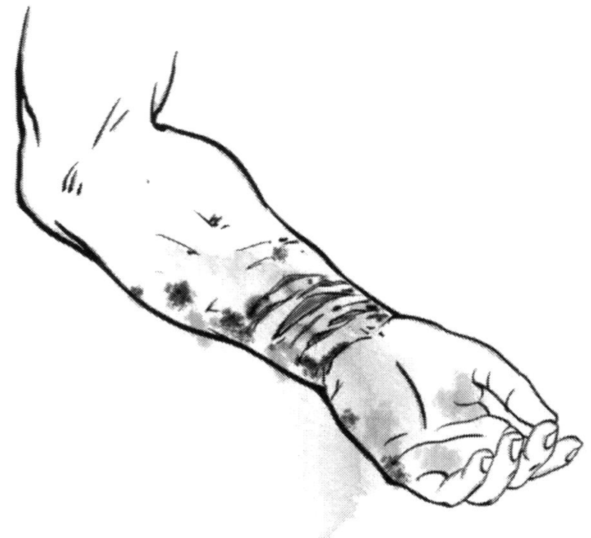

The tale of the sky and the ground always seemed so beautiful; the sky would always see the ground looking back at her... Despite the people that walked all over him every day. The ground saw that the sky looked at her forever and always, during the day when she was covered, and during the night where she wore her jewels. A love so tender, a love so unmaterialistic; a love that never touched.

Hurt

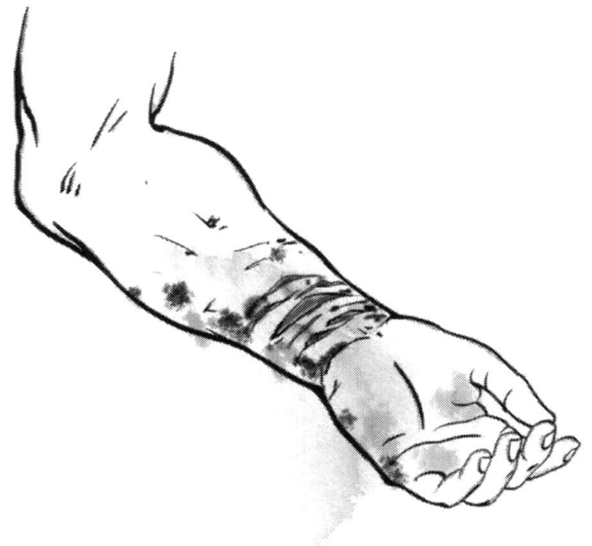

it often
feels like our heart
knows better
than what our mind
says;
but we know
that our mind
tries to save us
but our heart..
just doesn't
want
to
be
saved.

Hurt

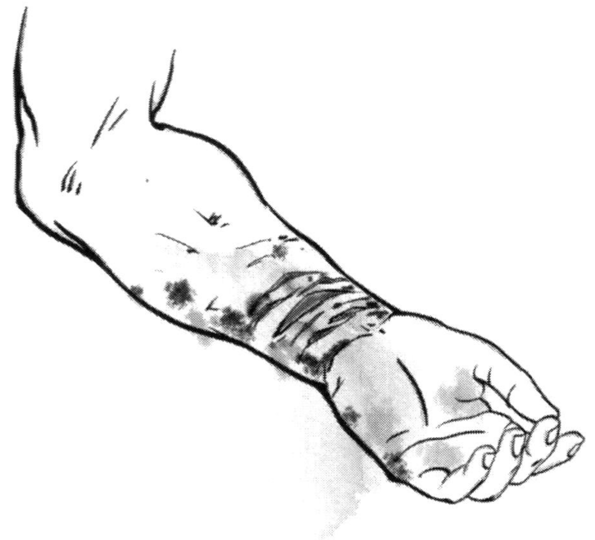

what i learnt
when i was younger
and was playful
and injured myself
daily
i bled, and bled, and bled
the wounds would heal, the scabs would stay
like a cover on the blood of frozen blood
the more i picked away at them
the more it hurt me
the more it felt satisfying
trying to take off something that
didn't fit with my body.
it would never fit.

-I like to think of being hurt like that, it hurts, you heal, but you don't want to heal. You want to bleed; you want to feel the pain that reminds you that you're still human. You begin to pick away at your mind until it leaves a scar that's visible to everyone... it becomes a part of you.

Hurt

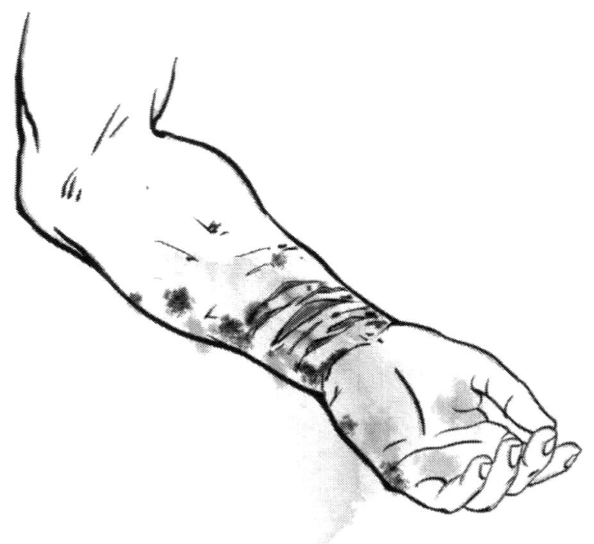

You try to run from pain, the more it catches up with you. You try to run from the past, but it's in every corner of every street. You drink, you smoke, you have sex, and you do what you do to forget it all... But it just doesn't seem to go away. It hurts, doesn't it? Trying to forget something that just doesn't seem to go away, no matter what you do. You drown yourself with the drinks, you suffocate yourself with the smoke. You smile through your mouth, but bleed from your eyes. You wish you could get away from it all.. Altogether. But a part of you just doesn't want to get away. This is you now, you don't remember a life outside of it.

Hurt

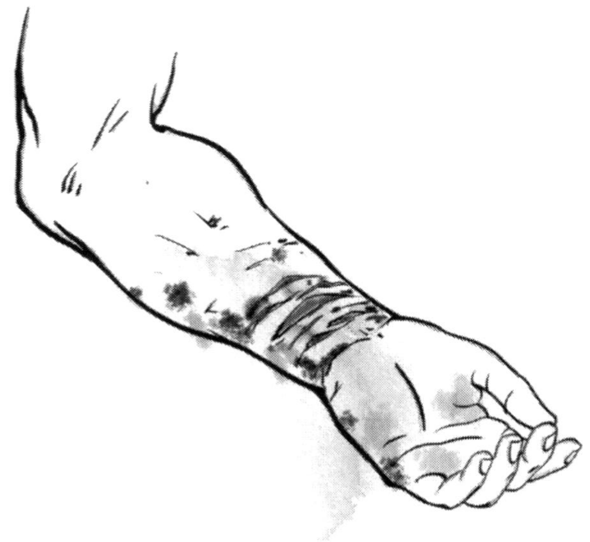

i don't love slightly,
i love with a passion
i don't give nothing,
i give everything
i don't like something a little
i obsess with it a lot
i fall in love with the darkest of places
and i swallow the light
so it flows from within.
i don't feel a little.
i feel a lot,
and when your heart is poured
onto the surfaces
of the depths of the walls
you see that it flows everywhere
even the places you never thought you'd
see.
and maybe that was my misfortune
to feel what i never did
to live with pain
i never imagined.

Hurt

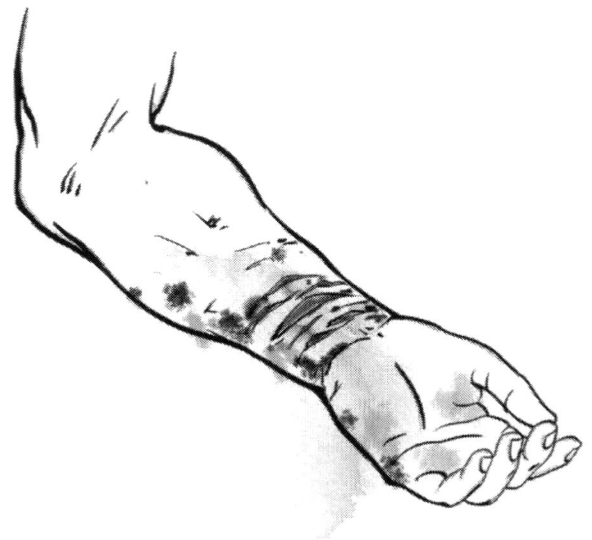

the worst kind of pain is the ones you can't explain. the type where you're struggling to crawl out the space of your heart, the type where you're not drowning, you're not suffocating… the one where you just don't know what's happening. your hands start to crumble, they start to shake when you try to reach for help, but you can't find it inside you to do so. you don't want to be helped. but you scream to be treated better, but it's like you're the only person listening.

Hurt

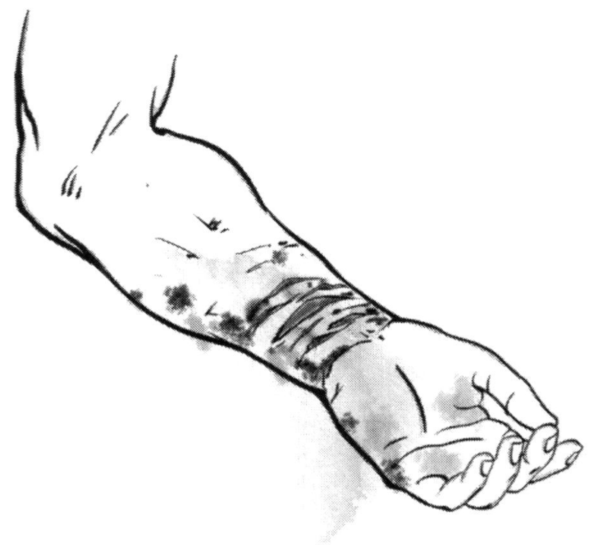

sometimes not being enough
not saying enough
not doing enough
hurts
but we live
and we learn
even waves calm
and they turn into
the tides
we see
when we drive past the shore
or stick our feet
into the sand
waiting for it
turn into mud

Hurt

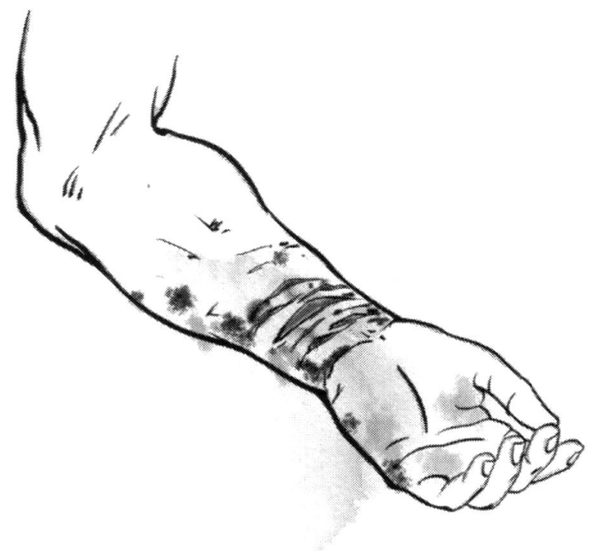

No one really knows what's behind the tears of a clown… a mask of laughter can only be broken down as much. It's the irony of smiling to only reveal a deeper energy, a deeper darkness that you want no one else to feel. A deeper worth that you feel that you don't want to be found, but rather to find other people, to bring out the beauty in themselves rather than reveal it to yourself. A clown only seeks the pleasure of amusing others, to make others feel better about themselves, while they live in irony, a life of opposites that only come off when the mask does. But the mysterious thing always has been how a person can only stay as sane, when they don't wear masks.

Hurt

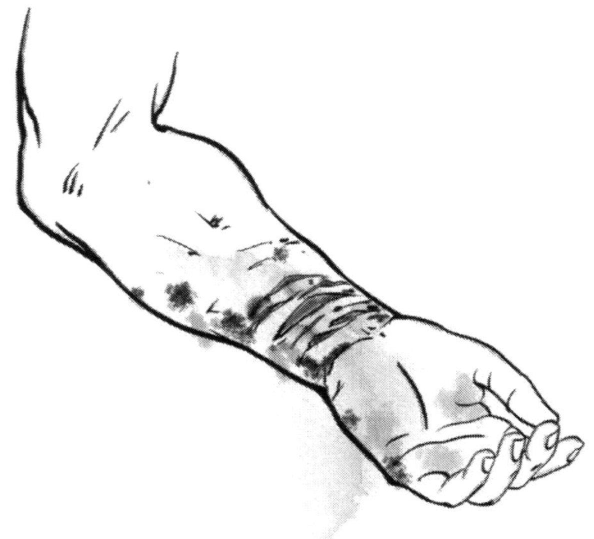

a million unspoken
words
a hundred thousand
feelings
a thousand
situations
a hundred
visions
a single
thought

-silence.

Hurt

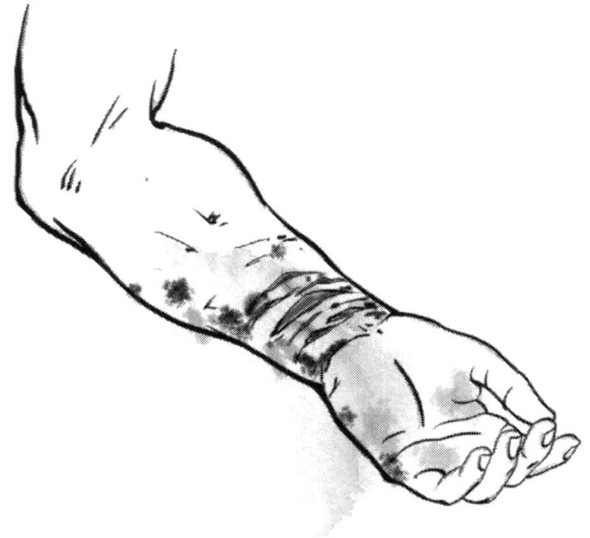

You just know those times, where you're just depressed for no reason, you just love and bask in the cloak of slow and sad songs, you just love the colour black, it's lifeless. Kind of like how you're feeling. You want someone to talk to you, about how you feel, you want to be comforted. However, that someone isn't that someone you want. It may sound fussy but hey, we're gonna die someday, no harm in being open about what you want. But you love it. You love and hate feeling like this, because you've never felt anything else, and this is the way you think you can express yourself in the deep dark abyss of being depressed. But that's not it. There's society. There's figures out there, models etc. who are sculptured to be the faces of today and tomorrow. You're depressed because you're not like them. You weren't blessed with good looks. You crave something you love, when you can't have it, you keep telling yourself that, leads to heartbreak and misery. Last but not least, the songs you listen to at night, the late night thoughts, being lonely in a world full of ghosts with beating hearts, leaves you with the concussion of a time bomb brewing in your mind, ready to explode your feelings all over the walls, but you're too strong for it, you keep telling yourself. All you allow past, is one measly tear and a fake smile, none know the tears of a clown. You feel alive when you're outside, yet you crave for someone you want to spend the rest of your life with, who's constantly on your nerves, but you love it. You crave it.

Hurt

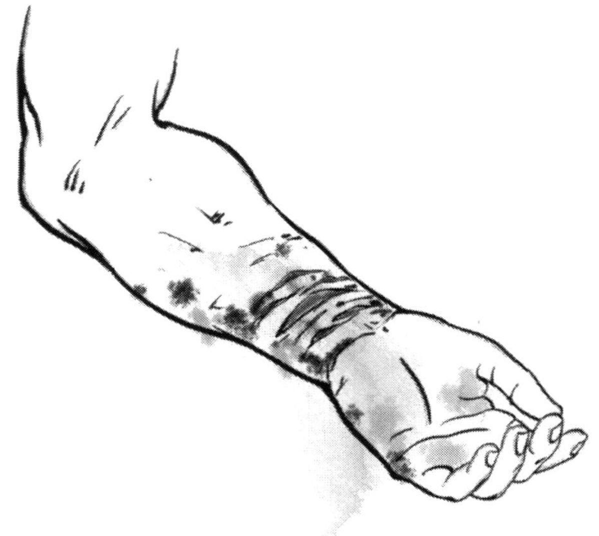

*the people you once
used to know
now live under your skin
inside your blood
as the ghosts
of the souls
you once thought
were entwined
to yours.*

Hurt

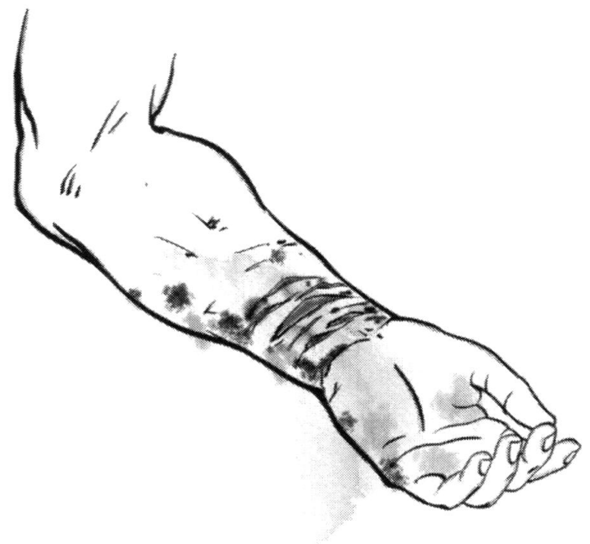

one of the biggest things that hurt the most
is not realising an opportunity when you see it
it is often dressed as misfortune
or rejection
and it is what destroys us
it leaves the heart
hanging onto the
sheer chance
that something beautiful
just passed by.

Hurt

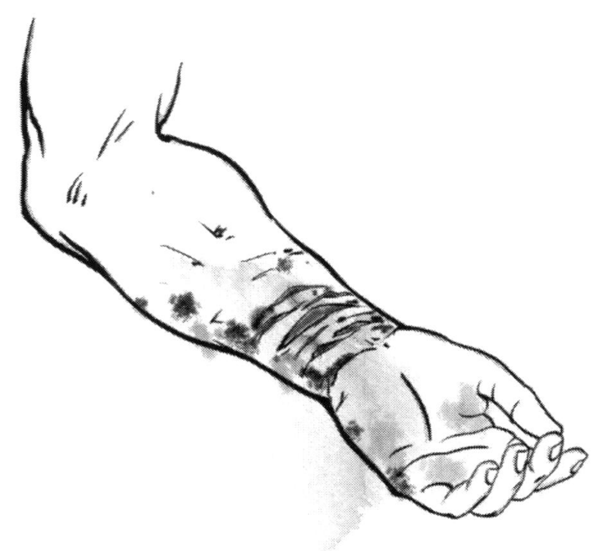

When you love
you love deeply
you change yourself
although you told yourself
you promised yourself
you'd never change.
you feel it surge in your body
you feel it surge through your veins
you forget who you were
and turn into what you are
and the thought of that
destroys the memories
of how you used to live.
all you have.. are memories
and when what you are
destroys you,
all you do

is turn into another memory of what you
used to be.

Hurt

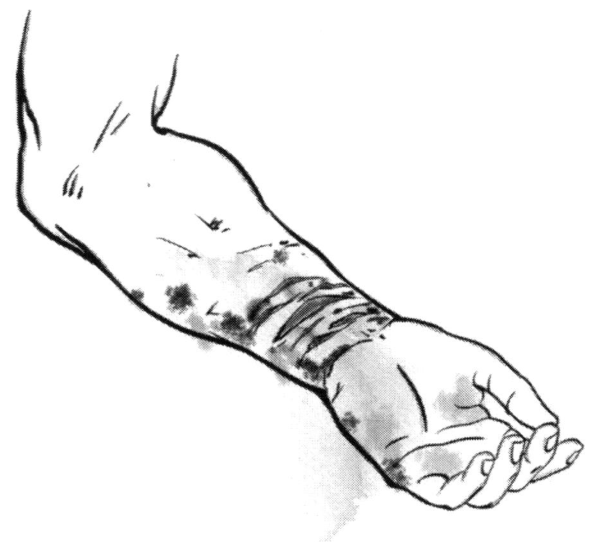

it will kill you
the sense of feeling useless
the way you think
that sometimes you don't have a purpose
it will eat away at you
and let you feel like
you're just a body into open existence
when the beauty is inside you

you feel like you're doing the wrong things
but what is inside you
doesn't match the reality you face
because two forces
that collide
have a greater power than the other.
what you feel
is time
throwing chances
at you
to be a better
you.

Yourself

maybe the thing about me
is that i get too attached
to things i find
are places i can hold myself
and be safe in
yet
most of the time
the places are beautiful
with danger signs polluted
all over the horizons.

Yourself

we confuse loneliness
with vulnerability
when vulnerability
is trapping yourself
into a state
where your emotions
your feelings are free
to be captive to anything
that extends its hands
to you.
loneliness
is the power
of concealing yourself
and learning more
about the world,
the tricks that opportunities play
of disguising themselves
as your enemies
when they only led you
to a place where
you could breathe
and your lungs
wouldn't fill
with toxic.

Yourself

One of the things I learnt about myself was that I was different... No, really, I was different. I spent a lot of time being someone I wasn't, years and years of trying to blend in to be someone that just wasn't me. A person made by society, following its norms and its values. I couldn't take it anymore. Thinking how everyone did, you would've thought I was a robot or something in a system full of errors who thought they were doing right in their own way. . . when really it was a trend they were following that enabled them to think that whatever they were doing was the right thing. We think accordingly to what would go on in people's minds despite whatever it is that we did. It's kind of like being trapped in your own body, with your mind as the guard with the keys; your heart is what you really want to chase, yet the mind thinks it all over too much, and too deeply that it doesn't make sense to your heart anymore, it's like a foreign language that doesn't make sense to you. . . but the more you hear it and try to feel what it really means, the more it makes sense. It's kind of like that with your mind, it doesn't make sense at first with the connection it has with your heart. . . but give it time. It'll start to make sense. . . and that's when you truly lose yourself. When the mind makes the connection with something, before your heart does. And that's what most people seem like nowadays, falling in love with something through their mind, not the heart... You might've heard of compatibility, then why do people not use their heart to feel, when it was made to do so? It's because when something's damaged too much, you prioritise it less. Lesser to not get it damaged anymore, you try and keep it safe. But no matter how hard you try, it'll always get involved, that's why they think first, learn first. . . rather than let their heart fall again. That's why people would rather pretend to be someone they're not, rather than be hurt for who they truly are. It's a facade. . . why lie to yourself when the truth is what's different to what others see?

Yourself

there is nothing
more poetic
than you.
to live
to breathe
to think
how you do
is all poetry.
and the way you'd see poetry
it was something that you'd read
and it'd make you think
it'd take you
to the places
of your mind
you'd forgotten about.

-you are poetry.

Yourself

you do not need to fit into society to be beautiful.

- a reminder for myself.

Yourself

It's always the littlest things that make the big things. Life will never have something big that wasn't small before. Growth is natural, everything big was small once; take you for example. You were once a cell. A cell that kept multiplying and multiplying to make you who you are today. Now imagine all your little habits, things that you do that you don't realise. You think that they're nothing... in someone's eyes, they could be the most beautiful thing they ever saw. It's just a matter of how you do it.

Yourself

you'll hate yourself for reasons you don't know
you'll hate people for judging you
when you are the biggest critic
your body can handle.
you wish you were someone else
anyone apart from yourself
you wish you were ripped of your negativity
and replaced with positivity
when you need to realise
the death of negativity
will always be positivity
in your mind
in your body
in your soul.

Yourself

there will be people in life
that will make you uncertain
and make you question
the loyalty
you show
which will always make you feel like
your energy was far lesser than theirs
but people do not have the same energy as you
and they never will
for a vibe like yours
can't be seen by the people
who've never felt what
you have.

Yourself

the most beautiful thing
about the people that always smile
is that they're fighting a battle
inside their soul
with a force that's
striking back
harder and harder
with each blow
but they rise
they rise higher
than the flames
of the damage inside them
to take over the fire that burnt them
to turn it into a silent flame
that hid in plain sight
but never made a sound.

Yourself

someday i shine differently
my true colours come out at night
i'm a different person every day
i show myself bit by bit
but i hide in the darkness most of the time
and some days
i shine brighter than i could ever imagine
but just as much as i shine
it doesn't take much to turn back
to the brightness
where the shining
is more hidden
than the darkest flame
in the hottest room.

Yourself

Have you ever noticed, how the more you search for something, the harder it is to find? But when you stop looking for it, it almost always seems to find its way to you? It's like whatever was meant for you wasn't yours to search for, maybe it had to find its way to you. Maybe you weren't meant to search, you were meant to be found, and maybe you saw what you were capable of doing, learning new things that you were given by the universe what you deserved?

Yourself

As you grow older, the things you really wanted, fade away. Like they weren't worth it anymore, like they lost that beautiful vision you had for them. You learnt that it wasn't what you needed to feel happy… you were looking for peace. Peace is the dream you were always chasing, not the materialism. You ever wonder whenever you'd chase something materialistic, you'd have that little moment of success, that little sense of relief afterwards, when you know you finally got what you wanted? That's peace. When you've finally got what you were searching for. Peace isn't laying on top of a building, looking for a shooting star in the middle of the night, with a cigarette in your hand. Peace is knowing that nothing can disturb you. Peace is knowing that you feel happy you feel nothing.

Yourself

there is only so much
you can do for people
and if you feel like
you dedicate yourself
to other people
than you do to
yourself
you will never
see happiness.

-you will wake up every day waiting for a chance to smile, a chance to open your eyes and follow your dreams… but realise that it hurts to look at yourself in the mirror, or even think something beautiful about yourself, simply because you chose to put people over yourself.

Yourself

how do you live with yourself
when the devils in your mind
pierce holes in your soul
rip apart the existence
of your heart
and tie you down
every time you
want to get up?

-existence

Yourself

When you think about life, you think about accomplishing all the biggest things in a short amount of time. I mean, who doesn't? It's great to say you did something big, something amazing in such a short amount of time, at a young age. To say that you were amazing, to say you're better than the rest. But then what happens? You look at yourself; you look in the mirror and see everything you ever hated staring back at you. You see your flaws; you see the two beautiful eyes staring back into your soul as if you were throwing knives at yourself. Knives with all of your flaws imprinted on them, like they were the brands shaped from what made them. And they all hurt more and more each time, with each knife hurt a different wound, with every wound, more you saw what was inside you and what did that bring? It made you feel naked, vulnerable. To the thought that you'll always be like this, when you look at yourself… you just feel useless; only because you're not doing great. What if I told you, that the most beautiful, the most lavish things in the world are only the ones that took time- I mean, look at you. There's only one of you in the world. Seven billion people, and there's you. Things take time, the best things just don't happen overnight, the idea probably does… but that's what makes it even better. You are made of flaws. Flaws that were meant to be embraced, flaws that could be your biggest power, instead of your biggest weakness. You aren't something to be ashamed of. You are everything to be proud of. Good things take time, and just because you aren't doing as much with your life as you think you are, there is always going to be another day. Where you'll wake up and think differently about how you're going to see the world.

Yourself

Trust only lies with whoever you leave it with. Trust? What is trust? Trust is giving someone a chance, not even a chance actually. Trust is giving someone the opportunity, the risk of putting you in danger. . . but also at the same time, holding you back from what has the power to kill us. You see, trust is something that has two sides, a dangerous side, and a safe side. We think of the safe side as some place we get to stay in, a place where it took us so long to get to, only to be taken away from it like it was nothing. But you see... When a person trusts you. . . they're vulnerable to you. It's like setting foot in the most beautiful house you've ever seen. But the other side of trust. . . is having to prove that you're worthy of it. You will face the hardest battles against yourself, with your ego and your loyalty- but that's the fuel for trust to run. Trust is putting your ego aside for someone to show you that not everything's the same.

Yourself

With us as people, we want to be saved. There's almost always a time and a place where we just fall into the category of just wanting to be saved. We say we want the world to explode, to burst into flames and for the world to suffer. I mean, it only seems logical when the world turns its shoulder on you, when the world just seems so reckless. But there is always that little glimmer of hope that you thought you drowned with all the alcohol or the smoke you inhaled into your body. There will always be that little spark of hope inside you that will never die… well of course, until you do. There's always hope that one day that the world will come to its senses and just open its doors to you. But it's all circumstances and situations that we're placed into that just influence our belief that things won't work out just by demotivating you that tiny bit more that ends up with you giving up with it practically. But the idea that it'll still happen remains with us mentally for a long, long time. And I think that's the most beautiful thing, how you think you've given up on something but it's somewhere hiding in the back of your mind just waiting for a time to come back out again.

Yourself

you drown yourself in the same sadness every day, just a little more each time. yet you still don't understand why it's difficult to breathe sometimes. we are the causers of our own pain.

Yourself

you
need
yourself
more than
people that
need you.
you
cannot be
a
foundation
when love
within yourself
is not present.

Yourself

we forget that
we do not belong to anyone
except ourselves
no one is allowed
into your soul
without you letting them in
and that way
it is the same
for when you're showing them
the same door
to leave.

Yourself

In life we learn that the most beautiful of things, weren't beautiful once upon a time. They were also once looking for the star in the night sky to lead them to the hope that one day they'll be up there, flying, catching everyone's attention too. Being there in the dark sky, with the glow that lit up the night sky, being the reason behind someone's deepest thoughts. We are not defined with the beauty on the outside; it's more to do with how a person can endure so much pain, so much suffering to be the ominous glow in the room that makes everyone wonder what your story is. The most beautiful of people have the ugliness in them, there's always a bad habit that haunts them every day, there's always a trace of negativity with the palms of positivity.

-A Bouquet Laced With Liquor.

To the reader
thank you for reading the parts of my mind I have yet to explore
and thank you for reading through sections of my mind
about how life works. What the main message from the book was, (if you haven't gathered already) was that everything isn't as it seems. People, materialistic things... They all have a deeper value, they all have a story to what made them... them. And I hope you enjoyed a venture into what was the most eye-opening adventure through my eyes and into my mind.

once again, thank you

-hvmz.h (Hamza Hussain)

22117185R10116

Printed in Great Britain
by Amazon